FIRSTMATTERPRESS
Portland, Ore.

ALSO BY ASH GOOD

These things will never happen quite like that again
I watch you find the sum in your obsession with a part (chapbook)
Years grew a keloid (chapbook)

SOUNDS IN MY MÖBIUS MIND

SOUNDS IN MY MÖBIUS MIND

ash good

FIRSTMATTERPRESS
Portland, Ore.

Copyright © 2018 by Ash Good
All rights reserved

Published in the United States
by First Matter Press
Portland, Oregon

Names, details and locations in this
work may have been altered to
protect privacy or may resemble actual
occurences, persons or places; these
stories are woven of poetic memory
and best regarded as fanciful

Paperback ISBN 978-0-9972987-5-8

Cover Illustration Copyright © 2016
by Holger Lippmann www.lumicon.de
Noise Scape 4 Series, generative digital art

Book design & typography
by Ash Good www.ashgood.design

FIRSTMATTERPRESS.ORG

my memories are my prayers

SOUNDS

prologue

13   or auntie spends hundreds of hours building the family tree

right now

19   i stop waiting for the perfect time

22   once i find my way / i'll remember how to sink right in

24   he says he'll expatriate then changes his mind like chelsea handler

26   the same thing that shapes wyoming mountains
     & soars seabirds

28   i know you're holy / my country doesn't care

30   when you see the future / it doesn't always happen

33   mama calls early with bad news

34   distracted from heaven by math & grilled pineapple skewers

36   mama texts late

37   i seek refuge at the goodwill later anyway

38   one paragraph of *the new yorker* / i jostle the
     anxiety monster free (again)

39   a picture of a past lover in a bikini on portugal sand / thinner than before

42   the violent repulsion of things / turning the word-spigot to a black hole

before that

49   in-between paydays / especially when daddy's habit beats mama to the bank

50   mama, jeffy & i go imagine new lives in double-wides

52   stillness can't be trusted / sea-legs bracing for what's coming

54   after the rain stops but before it gets hot / my favorite chore is burning

56   a voracious girlhood appetite / i wonder if i want to be the she or the he

57   you don't get to pick how it goes when you're a kid

59   slayed by el matador

60   it takes a key & code / to penetrate the walls of my castle

62	with folks i dig / homesick but already in california
64	her breakup note has a frida kahlo quote
67	after love / follow me home
69	i find mama's nightgown in a rubbermaid tub
70	three years learning to like the taste of beer / i drink a cold one with daddy
72	i wash my brother's feet / mama says he's on the spectrum
75	on the couch / i fit in the curl of mama's legs
78	mama's body hurts / call back what i am
80	maybe i'll run out of this kind of raw / then nothing will be left but god

then later

87	some shift happens / i note acutely each time i say woman
90	hourglass grains are gritty / in my rolls & creases
93	drive two hours north of seattle / to get to switzerland

97   i decide the trick to doing anything /
     believe i've done this before

100 i pray for a long time before i eat / mushrooms in moab

102 trans-religious significance / some long-stretching
     tendency toward holy

104 i say how have i missed this truth so long?

107 my hair smells like double bubble & mapacho

112 i cook breakfast twice / i kick over coffee while i meditate

115 it's different this time / moving only from that space

epilogue

119 or back again to the way it's always been

120 acknowledgments

PROLOGUE

OR AUNTIE SPENDS HUNDREDS OF HOURS BUILDING THE FAMILY TREE

story goes   my third-great-grandma   is a
                                    full-blooded german
      who marries a choctaw man
his mama who makes seven babies (or is it eight)   is nine
      in exile with her tribe
                on the trail of tears

                my great-grandpa is a coal miner
all my people ride out   in rickety automobiles
      from the dakotas & oklahoma
                        to the pacific

more than a fair share are criminals
            not much more to find in card catalogs
or online   i don't come from
      society pages

            i come from the eighties

where nothing important exists before
& now we know everything　　　　or will once they're done

　　　with that science study next year

　　　　　　　　　　　where not walking in front of
the screen　　is as holy as the sabbath
　　　　　　　　　　　　　　　blowing on nintendo games
　　　　　　　　　　　　is my ritual

i come from the eighties where the wisdom i get
　　　　　　　　　　　　　　is from my

lucky charms box　　　dutifully i pledge allegiance　　& knock out
　　　a hundred revolutions on my skip-it

long after some thing
destroys the yarn of my people—
　　　　　　　　　　　dirt poor white ones

　　　　　　　ravaged indigenous ones—

       i follow behind

                            dangling

    disconnected

             some wildly privileged baby
                                from the eighties

RIGHT NOW

> *"It is six a.m. and I am working.*
> *I am absentminded, reckless, heedless of social obligations, etc.*
> *It is as it must be. The tire goes flat, the tooth falls out,*
> *there will be a hundred meals without mustard.*
> *The poem gets written."*
>
> —MARY OLIVER

I STOP WAITING FOR THE PERFECT TIME

despite the mountain of motorcycle fairings in my
bedroom   & ice melting in the big white chest
in the living room   despite floors that badly need
vacuumed   instead of going to the goodwill to hound
plant stands or repotting roots over-watered then
moisture-starved while i am away

earlier in writing circle the deep feeling one reads about
a nobel laureate poet with two husbands & separate bedrooms
& i pray
         she's a sage seeing my future
                 some other place

i'll be something else
                     (likely missing
             some unquantifiable quality
         of what i am now—like that photo of us
     i keep in the bathroom that isn't really us anymore)

we've been living
         with a mouse   & where i crouch scribbling

      i note two droppings
by a shiny quarter (tails up)   near the closet mirror

the skin of my cheek is too rough   the laugh lines
too deep   perhaps i should wax those invisible glints
on my upper lip   *how can my lovers stomach all this?*
      sit straighter
           don't slouch

find the place where the matter   doesn't matter
until it flows at the spine & out clear eyes   where i know
      before vacuuming   i should come here

don't ever stop writing   she says
      the deep feeling one
          who pens down my impending self
              don't ever stop

when she pulls away she sees— *you couldn't could you?*

      later i am juggling
two backpacks at LAX   when she rings to say

    something happened to me   *i can hear the trees cry*
i'm going now   *i only thought i should tell someone*
              who understands

ONCE I FIND MY WAY / I'LL REMEMBER HOW TO SINK RIGHT IN

in the closet is a perfectly good wardrobe
                                                    i feel like a fraud in
a costume mishmash of

—the lace tights of echo park's   low-light hipster dens

—a long phase of mammoth men's dress clothes—cashmere
         sweaters & silk button-downs—i hide in when my shapes get
slimmer   from the curves of being woman
                from the committal   of gender

—neutral woven hemp & organic cotton   left over from healing
      circles & astral projection &
                                     feigning softer than i am

when i look up & want a selfie—   to record
                the reflection of this rough skin
needs-to-be-washed hair   & salmon cuffs—
                          i wonder if frida kahlo is visiting

look at this she screams   *look at this raw*   *flawed*
          miraculous thing

os points at it once—my body—when we are out of them
        on a spaceship crafted from a red door motel
  room   in the in-skirts of long beach
                                        he points & says

                you made that

when i look down i say

          i'm going to need another one of these

most of the time this flesh dwarfs me—
                        not fully in

    spelunking for the nimble cavern
                              of a fingertip
rooting for the crater depths
                of these hips

HE SAYS HE'LL EXPATRIATE THEN CHANGES HIS MIND LIKE CHELSEA HANDLER

november ninth in the plains of kansas   in my (immodest?)

yoga pants & purple reversible
     vest & nike trainers & that flat-billed
          cyan & hot pink leopard
     print hat nu finds for me at the goodwill
       in clarksville tennessee

in the shell market while the tank fills up   i search for
     salvation   in lenticular postcards
   & plastic keychains
i give up finding comfort
          on convenience store shelves

big men pile in carharts on tiny tables   a booming *oh-bah-ma*
     drifts with me out the door

i squat on the curb & take a drag off this
          american spirit

i wonder what i am in this world
         pretty? possessable? inconsequential?
   dangerous?

nu crosses the lot toward me   those farmers & truckers
        can't tell from his face   that he's muslim—
                his last name's hussein

down the freeway nu unfurls me
                from the passenger seat
i heave to say
        it's not casual conversation for me—
            the thought of not making home
                      with you

it's just words he says   *i'm probably*
    not really going to leave   *you know it's just words right?*

he holds me until i'm calm
                along our 'mericuh veins

THE SAME THING THAT SHAPES WYOMING MOUNTAINS & SOARS SEABIRDS

in jackson hole the tourists have all gone home
the slatted boards of the coffee shop porch
                                             are diamond cold

i kneel to take a picture   of ice under his adidas

          we drive
since last sunday   through atlanta & the torched smokies

pause for live acoustics
                              escape kansas

                teetering corners
                     to pike's peak

                            in all the places   i stop still
lay down flat   stare back at where its pouring out

                          travel in instead of around

            travel out

    the year before
                this time on the road
                              i go shake every sunday

cocooned in healing chants
    a few
              show up   so it   moves us

      pulses in fits & starts   until
      lit up
             my hand trembles
                          & i lay it on him

I KNOW YOU'RE HOLY /
MY COUNTRY DOESN'T CARE

we pass a german man who passes us then
                stops to talk at a gas station
                              he thinks
the election results won't change anything here   *but in europe*
he says   *everything always changes*

i see two f-sixteens over eighty-second   banking hard left
toward the airport

i never see war
        but we fight one on TV since i am seven

i never see war
        but have no choice but to live off its profits everyday

it's the last writing circle for winter when i ask the deep feeling one
    if i might
                hug her   i cup her face whole
      in my hands to say
  the depth of your feeling is impeccable   *& it's seen*

the wall between our eyes pitches

        oh!
              you do see me

      my courage runs like stockings i don't wear anymore
i bolt from the eternity well of   split-second merger
    into my boots at the door
        ready to flee
                jolted by intimacy

WHEN YOU SEE THE FUTURE / IT DOESN'T ALWAYS HAPPEN

back to bed   i lie on my back
      in a small pop tendons stretch
    across skull   os drapes himself over me

my hand rests in his hair when the pulse starts up & down
      my spine   releasing   spinning
          i feel it arc
through my palm into him   it's in both of us
              the stuff that floats underneath
& explodes out from the center   to make everything
      rumbling steadfast

            a sizzling kettle with a broken bell—
            it should be ringing now

the walls shake   the roar grows
      but my eyes are closed   os still over me—

i want to move but can't   i need to move
but can't   this quake goes until nu opens a door

a dimension collapses
      & i wake   still flat

      still pulsing
           still safe

      my fingers in soft hair

so ellie won't stop talking about earthquakes &
    it isn't helping my anxiety says jesse lynne

how does ellie know about earthquakes?
(it's weird   things three year olds start to know)

i'm not sure but when we pull up to mcdonald's to play
she tells me we can't go in there   there's going
    to be an earthquake

jesse lynne is terrified
of the oregonian-made-mythic cascadia tremor

    set to crumble every foundation
        where jaunting over bridges
                is our way of life

months ago i meet

      a man who reads the i ching & tells me he knows

          it is going to happen
          in two weeks

when that day comes   nothing happens

      i haven't had tea with him again   to see
          how he feels about that

MAMA CALLS EARLY WITH BAD NEWS

mama tells me
        that when she tells dawn-marie—

my wide-eyed
fair-haired niece—that her baby brother
              is dead
      she tears up angrily & says

              but gammie
i've already lost two family members—

         my great grandpa & my papa rick

            & at least four fish

DISTRACTED FROM HEAVEN BY MATH & GRILLED PINEAPPLE SKEWERS

i park my van where it's easy
    & get in mama's car   jeffy is smoking a cigarette
        dawn-marie is watching youtube tweens
mama is bent over the rear floorboard
                gathering kernels
    & stomped soda cups—   her spaces
        hesitant to release

at brunch dawn-marie orders apple juice
            but promptly declares it apple cider
    eight-year-olds know these things

halloween is five days away   dawn-marie tells me
    my sissy is going to be batgirl
        & my mom isn't dressing up
            & my daddy-david is going to be batman
                & i'm going to be a husky—

        her pause is long

& my brother was going to be robin
but now he's—   she stops

& just points up

we didn't even get to show him
what halloween is

it's quiet for a long time before jeffy says
you know what i think we need to do soon?
go to brazil grill

well you better start saving daddy!

her brain runs off to calculate three grown-ups'
& one kid's entry to her favorite south american
all-you-can-stuff-your-face eatery

thirty-nine plus thirty-nine plus thirty-nine

MAMA TEXTS LATE

    baby girl has had several meltdowns but now
    we're cuddling & watching a show
    she sure is asking some hard questions

        the big questions   mama—
        no one knows the answers to those

    that's what i told her—
    some things we don't know

i toke & sink long on the floor
a pulse of watching in my center—tight & weary & worked

                breathe there
      be as big as you are

          you're big enough for today

I SEEK REFUGE AT THE GOODWILL LATER ANYWAY

to search for afghans
        for a new rug to go in front of the door
                for a robe (i find one that's rainbow)
    to wear on the polar express with mama & jeffy & dawn-marie

i find a pair of patagonia leggings
        two jean jackets i don't buy
i stand for a long time wearing a part angora
      shrug   (made in korea) studded with pearls
            & synthetic garnets   down the lapels
i daydream
        of living in this wool   for winter
but i can't get over fifteen percent acrylic & barely there

      stains   at the nape
                      when i'm brought back by the sound
of a fighter jet passing over

      costumes futile

             in this roar of war things

ONE PARAGRAPH OF *THE NEW YORKER* / I JOSTLE THE ANXIETY MONSTER FREE (AGAIN)

i google radiation suits a few weeks ago
then when i tell nu he laughs in my face
this is the world we're coming to
the type where i feel the sudden need

to know everything about radiation suits
(a decent bargain really at fifteen hundred dollars)
while i sit in traffic on ninety-second to get to trader joe's
to buy groceries for christmas dinner

nu tells me *it wouldn't work   besides*
i still want one

A PICTURE OF A PAST LOVER IN A BIKINI ON PORTUGAL SAND / THINNER THAN BEFORE

i am convinced there is a balloon in my body
        i ask myself if
                my eyes are saying this & i just can't see right again
        or if i feel it from the inside

i worry about the welt on my left cheek that is maybe a hive
        from almonds i sabotage myself with
or perhaps a bug bite   like i also find on my hip

but i am more concerned that it's the start of another age mark
that it will grow rough & brown
                which is only problematic

because it is directly opposite one on my right cheek

when we say symmetry of the face is beautiful
        this is not   what we mean

i am asked to lay & meditate with an upper arm aware
        of a near stranger   whose lover leaves them
with peach-bruised neck skin   three days healed now
                crescent shapes

i can't stop the judge   from reaching conclusions

      i can't stop the judge   from turning on me

this morning that same place on my opposite arm is
      against cool gunmetal   nu keeps loaded
        since his time in the navy
            tucked in the futon crease next to his head

after i go to his room & under the duvet where
      he moves over for me without opening his eyes
        & we don't take off our clothes
until we both shut off alarms twice
      egg yolks should already be over medium

then tonight
when it's after seven i take a warm salt bath
        but everything is still off

the size of my thighs   the water drop on the back of my arm
            that has insect legs

    the notion that this is passing discontent

                                        there is nothing to fix

            is in the air   or under my skin

fat is power

                i hear my teacher say

                      & surely she means energy

                                kilocalories stored for locomotion

but grateful in some fleeting moment

                                    to feel

                                          i have so much

THE VIOLENT REPULSION OF THINGS / TURNING THE WORD-SPIGOT TO A BLACK HOLE

i resort to the old way   i'm the last one awake
i dial the screen down then
the last click off so it's just me & the keys
       that tap
              thoughts smoothed by

fingers that know what to do   at least something
     knows   i've been anxious   & annoyed
         i webmd annoyance depression
    unconvinced a label helps

       well   that is unexpected—os leaps

from the floor   barely makes it to the sink to retch
i should keep writing
          there is always an excuse

but i stop to put an ice pack on his neck
                        douse vomit filled
dishes in searing soap   tetris the dishwasher
run a bath & hope   it makes him feel

better   i am distracted by my phone
his podcast grunting down the hall

                        the whirlpool death
      rattle

                        i wonder if he is done?   if the hot water is
gone?   he's back in the kitchen with no time to say
     he's about to be sick again

                                at least the sink is empty

he sways over the drain
                i go for the compress   he turns the water
          on

                like the times i hold him & nu
    while they get   time-travel-sick

like the time he holds back   my box-died black strands
          under golden arches in an eagle
rock parking lot   after an unfortunate evening of
              sake

          my face aches over my right eye   he rustles
          an engine sounds

                i wince at my words
pallid & worn out
                bob ross exalts happy little
        trees   netflix auto-plays seven episodes

    we fade in & out of sleep

BEFORE THAT

"She dropped her shyness like a nightgown, and in the liquid glare of sunlight on old boards she held up her hands . . ."

—GREGORY MAGUIRE

IN-BETWEEN PAYDAYS / ESPECIALLY WHEN DADDY'S HABIT BEATS MAMA TO THE BANK

i feed sticky cans into the deposit machine & pour
                a heavy jar down the throat of a coin-star

definitely okay & not too desperate
                mama's picking through the silver

before we head into town to save one each
                of the new state engraved quarters

in her cardboard booklet   pressing serrated
                edges into reserved crescents

MAMA, JEFFY & I GO IMAGINE NEW LIVES IN DOUBLE-WIDES

from the first crack   of the door   the glue smells
like new shoes &   again we have to tell jeffy

          to stay on taut   plastic paths

on pristine floors   while he sprints off to claim
               a bedroom   he'll never move into

i'm picky about colors   mama is picky about
      if the space feels   divided in two

we marvel at sunken tubs
      with jets   & powder fresh drywall

if we want to look at more
      we drive the rest of the way to rainier—
to the nicer lot   with triple-wides & chainsaw
              carvings of bears

we don't notice cheap fixtures   or hollow doors

we compromise about how   *yes*   *the bedrooms*
      in this one are smaller   *but we could make do*
          & just look at that closet space!

but we don't get new closets

we stay in the farm house where
                daddy grows up with the oil heat

      & the dingy kitchen floor   mama scrubs
        over & over on her hands & knees but
                never looks clean

with the brown carpet   & second floor bedrooms
      under slanted ceilings where

we can't stand tall   asbestos wall boards
      & no closets   for keeping what's ours

STILLNESS CAN'T BE TRUSTED / SEA-LEGS BRACING FOR WHAT'S COMING

when it's good i hide under blankets
        with a flashlight & speed read   far past
lights out to the rattle   of mama & daddy's
       yahtzee dice   or the battery-fed

robot voice   that sinks battleships

       when it's not good there's screaming

snarls   a slam

              after the night away

panicky because   maybe   daddy will hurt himself
    this time   maybe   mama won't ever   forgive him

but this morning

gran talks in a sing song &
        wipes snail trails from jeffy's   coke-bottle lenses
like nothing happened

                no fight   no threats
    no gun   no taco dinner left out uneaten

    when i get home from auntie's
the straw stack of yellow
                cheddar sweats on a counter

AFTER THE RAIN STOPS BUT BEFORE IT GETS HOT / MY FAVORITE CHORE IS BURNING

but we don't burn garbage only cardboard
  & a three month old christmas tree
  newspaper coupons that don't get spent
  torn open envelopes phone books

for nineteen-ninety-five nineteen-ninety-six
only on burn days only with a burn permit

usually in the oil barrel that lasts three years—
    new & black & shiny
  next to the last one rusty & burnt through
  & the one before that crooked & dissolved

late in spring the pile has been growing since the final frost
  there's trimmed branches hefty bags of pepsi boxes
      stowed in the wood shed

it's dry enough now that it will catch & so i can declare
        (if i time it right) that i am going to burn
        & perhaps get out of doing dishes
        or picking up towels on the bathroom floor

but only to responsibly light things in the barrel
& poke at it with a stick to let in oxygen

heat waves push back my face
        the first whisper & hiss of some elemental witch

A VORACIOUS GIRLHOOD APPETITE / I WONDER IF I WANT TO BE THE SHE OR THE HE

i devour every scrap of letter-chatter in sight
        cereal boxes   flyers   newspapers   the merck manual
that lives in the bathroom   books   every book in the house

i hide in books for babies & new readers & young
        adults & mama's boxes of creased & worn romance
smut passed between her & her four sisters & daddy's

magazines that also live in the bathroom but are not
        so easy to find—glossy eighties rags boasting greased
up barely-not-teens with pussies pulled wide

i read about the girl at the drive-in who crawls in the bed
        of a pickup & under the cover of an old canopy begs
to be spanked until her round cheeks are numb &

apple-pink   i read about the trim lady jogger with pert
        nipples cutting her sheer white top who follows
into the stockroom late at the corner-market to be

fucked strung across grapefruits & have oversized
        zucchini plunge deep between swollen labia so
you can never stock the produce the same way again

YOU DON'T GET TO PICK HOW IT GOES WHEN YOU'RE A KID

the bathroom is small   & a pile of molding
       that doesn't get reinstalled
             after a half-ass remodel years ago
         piles precariously   in the crack
            behind the door   finish

nails spike in every direction   stick-on linoleum tiles don't
      quite reach all the way   behind
         the toilet
         stop short square
         around the curve
         of the tub

a paper corner of tropical fish trim wilts from the wall

aftershave & used razors   & half-empty 99-cent shampoo
      bottles   spill from a press board shelf

         the sink scum is daddy's whiskers   & our toothpaste

spit   i fill the flimsy dixie cup with scalding tap water
                        & watch the steam

                        i flip it against   skin i hate

                            to feel something

SLAYED BY EL MATADOR

i think you'll do just fine he says with an arm hanging
        out the window of my beat blue wagon
                i mean you're pretty smart—

it doesn't really matter where you come from
        i'm not sure why i confess so much to a stranger
                i only see twice

it's quiet for the rest of the drive to el matador
        we hide in a bite-size curl of sea cave
                i bury black polish in sand

& watch pretty girls wearing as little as i wish i was
        he pulls off his shirt & runs for the waves
                it's october & cold water shivers over his tan

later when my shirt comes off
        he doesn't really kiss me
                anymore   but he says

well all those marks on your belly
        they're a lot like the sun shining
                on the bottom of the ocean floor

IT TAKES A KEY & CODE / TO PENETRATE THE WALLS OF MY CASTLE

> "But I'll tell you what hermits realize. If you go off into a far, far forest and get very quiet, you'll come to understand that you're connected with everything."
>
> —Alan Watts

that safe one-bedroom sprawls between
        landscaped courtyards where i only see neighbors

the professional young couple who occasionally pass
        in their naval officer uniforms
              i miss she is growing a human

until i see them again when i'm on acid with eyes wide
        like her gestitating belly & the only time in four years
            i speak to her i say

        oh man! you're having a baby!
            she nods   *it's terrifying*

i leave my castle to hunt
        for tea cups to plant cacti in so i can name them
            napoleon & marie antoinette

but mostly i leave to spy on other worlds
        the mid-century home with the pristinely-trimmed grass
                that isn't astroturf (i check)   & one single flamingo
            plus four neon orange signs
                to keep off the lawn

        all belonging to that lady   cross & frail
                i see only once hurrying indoors

also the overpass in the other direction
over the busiest freeway in the biggest metropolis in the west

        i stick my nose through the chain link fence

feel a cool metallic taste press into my lips

still for an hour in the wind
                some perdurable mess   of universes

WITH FOLKS I DIG / HOMESICK BUT ALREADY IN CALIFORNIA

    limp & warm & sinking   against three lovers
        on the sofa i make   by folding two memory
    foam mattress toppers
           &covering them with a duvet   shoulder

    blades on the wall   chins topple   eyes close   or
        maybe open   barely
              in front of the lilies in the vase
       on the budweiser trunk
                in front of the sony trinitron
with kerchunk buttons
            i buy from a man
              in the valley
                  hold on my lap all the way

        there are three-foot speakers cooing

          i don't remember if
    we just smoke weed or take something

                            a perfectly
                  preserved sliver   convinces me
we're the holiest   we'll be

                      what if we just die like this?
                          twenty-seven

sublime   they find us later   him & him &

     her & me   entombed in joni

but we don't die
     & other things happen on that couch

like the time i turn to kelp   floating green with
                    light shining   straight through me

     or when i cajole him into giving me
          that dulcimer   i never play

HER BREAKUP NOTE HAS A FRIDA KAHLO QUOTE

i am going to go to the soaking pools
at esalen with her   in the middle of the night
         under moonlight   when riffraff can get in
but now some friend she is going with   isn't keen on bringing
strangers from the internet   so i don't & all i have
       is memory imaginations   of us sprawled there

handsome as steve mcqueen   in that black & white
       photo i save to my desktop
                i meet her instead
for a show at a gallery   she parks a subaru downtown
       in a tight spot   leaves me a little impressed
i'm shy   with a plastic tumbler of white

wine   she's a head shorter than me   wide dark
      eyes   hair half-shaved   flowing   thick &
black out the other side   she's the third girl i ever
        go on a date with   i don't think she knows   is this
a date?   we walk across concrete blocks   straight
      for little tokyo   when i look up humming

halogen in this joint is covered   in plastic
        prints of rolls & sashimi   in the courtyard there's
a wishing tree   i take photos of red lanterns against
        purple sky   she takes photos of me   i beat her
at air hockey   she beats me at pong   & we ride
        a quarter-operated merry-go-round   i take a picture of

a virgin mary   holy glowing in a window   framed
        in rainbow hanging beads   she eats shrimp
cocktail & tells me about how many virgin marys
        her mama has   & about the virgin mary in sequins
on a beach towel that weighs eighty pounds
        her mama insistently sends home with her once

on a plane   the same night she tells me about her
        mama's virgins   she tells me about how she was
conceived in a holy grotto   *like for real—that's why
        she named me love*   at the park with the spaceship
where we have a vegan picnic   she takes a
        picture of me in skinny jeans   & moccasins

draped in a silk men's dress shirt   reigning over houses
          built for sims   i don't know if i ever
touch anything as soft as the part of her   that stretches
          over her chest plate   where ink in black old english says
love conquers all   (in latin)   i don't know if i ever touch
          anything as delicate   as the bump of her wrist where

i rub out tension she winds up   retouching past
          midnight   when she's in my stories
someone in my crit circle notes   underlined   *love*
          what a loaded choice for a name!
like i just decide to give her   this perfect name
                    i find her with

AFTER LOVE / FOLLOW ME HOME

in this near empty river house
                in love's upstairs bedroom
a wool pendleton throw
        with three primary stripes   folds over
the end of the bed   she lights sage
                os settles in   by my leg

        a fog horn bellows
                where it's white   from columbia
mist & wolf moon light   the courthouse clock toll
        vibrates   my spine

next to the alley between   the old-towne theatre
        & boarded-up   association
        of pulp & paper   workers
            where   os scampers up
            narrow walls   like spider-man

a long time   after the time
      when gramp leaves
        everyday for graveyard   with his pail
as smoke stacks go &
        stench barely registers   in my mill-town nose

                this afternoon   at the
            forest temples it's all normal until the
        trunks eclipse the sun   & a portal opens

    we take pictures   of us taking pictures
            of light that splays from   an unlatched door
    but we stay here   where i almost love love
            & love almost loves me

            we meditate
    in a circle   no one leads   until we look up
            finished at the same time &
                    there's a singing bowl   she chimes

I FIND MAMA'S NIGHTGOWN IN A RUBBERMAID TUB

in the overflowing hallway
        the same satin i reach out   to touch
                                              when i am small

every time i pass through their bedroom door
after i watch the jetsons upstairs with daddy till after
noon when

        the slit of a retractable vinyl shade spills
        dust rays on wood floor & then it's too warm

i steal mama's blue romper i wear that whole summer

plus that nightgown

        robin's egg with a deep v-neck
            lined in cream lace that stretches over
                my grown-up collar
                    bones

THREE YEARS LEARNING TO LIKE THE TASTE OF BEER / I DRINK A COLD ONE WITH DADDY

record breaking i say & point out the glass
        to the overflowing flower pot   auntie squints at
           & pretends to see

      the clouds have been sobbing for two & a half days

i join them driving away on a quarter tank with mama's gas
        money in my pocket   it's hard to tell if the bleary lines
          require a higher setting for the wipers
              or the back of my hand

past the place daddy calls *the dirty thirty*
      where the red door with a life-size mudflap girl
          invites men done at five to park
    off the fog stripe for a night tucking
              dollars into panty lines

i think back thirteen miles to being inside daddy's favorite bar
      where his friends always say they see the resemblance

            it's been that way since he adopts me
when i am two   but already speak in complete sentences

every time this happens i shake their hand & laugh loud (like him)
            but they don't know why we're laughing

jeffy does have daddy's jeans—levi arches stitched on 501 pockets—
      but also his DNA   daddy's gait & the way
            their jaws are set

the nature crawls out of jeffy   down to the cross
      of their long
            thin legs   high across the knee—left toes
    nervous & bouncing a white new balance

I WASH MY BROTHER'S FEET / MAMA SAYS HE'S ON THE SPECTRUM

> *"If then, the lord and the teacher washed your feet,*
> *you also ought to wash one another's feet."*
> —John 13:14

i count out the change from my cider & jeffy's IPA
        & hand him the forty he asks to borrow

distracted by dark pores on his neck—
        i remember bribing him so i can pick at his skin

with a comedone extractor i learn about in *seventeen*

back way before then when he's three feet tall & porcelain
        he is my first love   towheaded in his race car waterbed
        begging me *sissy please just read go dogs go again*

when we get home from the bar i say *clean feet   clean socks*
        he doesn't protest   like he's still seven & i am nine

in my bathroom he finds the pliers to turn on the faucet
    i roll his jeans into wide cuffs pushed
        high on hairy calves

get in there i say pouring epsom salt & dr bronner's

i scrub between toes
    too quickly to assess (for my own good)
    if black spots are mildew or lint

i know i should take better care of my feet

fully clothed he stands in an inch of warm water
    i dig in a mason jar on the sink for silver clippers

you have to be careful
    my feet are ticklish

i trim off claws that bend 'round the ends
    i rub on lavender & tea tree oils

i tell him to dry it all real well

is that what will keep them from smelling?

i mean with feet like yours that sweat a lot buddy
        i think you just need to change your socks a few times a day
        like when you wake up—

& when i go bowling?
        i could just always keep clean socks in my bowling bag
        for when i put bowling shoes on
                —i go bowling almost every day

ON THE COUCH / I FIT IN THE CURL OF MAMA'S LEGS

i lift a thick stack of drawings from a tin they're treasured in
a single ballpoint line on each knots itself
        to make a street scene
                a man with a cowboy hat
                      a long-nosed sedan

mama talks aloud about working two jobs   two months after
      she has me   driving her chevy luv to the taco bell
& the trucker diner   where a man comes for coffee
      & leaves her these all-in-one-line sketches
            on a napkin   or the back of the receipt

how it's one hundred & nineteen in the shade   that summer i come
        (two years before we marry daddy)   & we hole up
      in the house
           & only go out under stars

further back how her favorite high school teacher takes the whole class
        to water ski in a pyramid on a plywood board

that awful date her own mama makes her go on
        with the boy from church   who spills beer all over her
          & refuses to drive her home
                so mama calls her two best friends

        (boys she never kisses) to come rescue her

& how later one of those boys dies when he is hit by a train
        she pulls up her grey sweats to point at the spongy scar
            from when she almost dies herself
                in a country highway head-on

    how a fluffy white sheep dog wakes mama up   in a house blaze
        that quits college for her when she can't afford
                              to replace burnt books

& some twenty-three hours of hard labor
                alone in a paradise maternity ward
    she follows with how
        i'm the best thing that ever happens to her

MAMA'S BODY HURTS / CALL BACK WHAT I AM

> *"I have begun to listen to the teachings my blood whispers to me."*
> —Hermann Hesse

if i barely push
        my finger into the soft part   of her upper arm
she winces   i feel the masses
       of tangled muscle   around the blades
along the vertebrae   she says i know

just where to find them   i feel the stirring inside
        of healing hands

splay out my knees & there
      screaming from released sinew

i can't deny
        i know   before i come here
                  i am a healer again & again

so i start inviting them back
        & in the place before sleep

these hands smooth the straps of my neck
      unfurl my resistance

i call them back   when i look in the mirror

        & faces appear

          drawn from time

      these healers i am   i remember them

so they rise from the crease of my thigh
              & spill out my mouth

        these healers inside

MAYBE I'LL RUN OUT OF THIS KIND OF RAW / THEN NOTHING WILL BE LEFT BUT GOD

i read about a guru's   ink-brimmed notebooks   but when you
    crack them open   it just says god inside

sanskrit scrawl

        ram   *ram*   *ram*   *ram*

he sits everyday   to write
    & all that comes out of him is   god

    my pen cuts   from those years
    daddy's lost in glass   in denim with a gun
    out in the back   aiming for rats

    while mama begs   for his coat
    to come off   just for an hour
    so she can   wash it

i arrive late   to letting this memory go

    the flower moon is full

    since 2:42 yesterday   with no time for ritual
          she wanes now—barely—still craving fire

    with fingers
that smell of a man & me   i mummify the dead fly—

    done circling—
in a holy white square   wings crinkle
      at my timid touch

i gather the mobiles of past connection

        lay oak spinners
tied with string in a pyre i tent
published pages over   i add the fly my blood
        the snake skin

dry & dusty i find two summers ago
in a cow pasture on sauvie island   i stand up the last
inch of that rainbow-tied   sage stick—

anoint everything

with almond oil (which doesn't light dramatically   like i envision)
swelling drops erupt dandelion orbs

my smoldering notebook page reads
                may my sorcery only be   liberating
                        in all beings' highest good i ask these things

i probably do this magic wrong
                i offer my pain to the mother
     gods
                      a stick snaps under my foot

THEN LATER

*"I cure with Language. Nothing else.
I am a Wise Woman. Nothing else.
I am wise even from within the womb of my mother.
I am the woman of the winds,
of the water, of the paths,
because I am known in heaven . . ."*

—MARIA SABINA

SOME SHIFT HAPPENS / I NOTE ACUTELY EACH TIME I SAY WOMAN

> *"I find myself drawn to feminine archetypes that previous generations have found threatening or dangerous: crones, oracles, madwomen, amazons, virgins who aren't helpless..."*
> —Catherynne M. Valente

on the shore of the willamette after paddling up current
    a girl stranger & her mom are there with a dog
she is slender & tall   wearing a black bikini—

not really a girl   somewhere past the cusp of woman
    but not beyond the threshold where girl becomes insult

she probably still calls herself one like i do—
    into my thirties still unsure of claiming

        some power i store dormant

soft blond strands glint in river sun above the bone of her ankle
    on the definition of her quad

in the car yesterday i talk aloud

    why do i always remember this stray hair
        when i don't have tweezers & forget about it
            when i do?

now my circles become undeniably women—
            some place supplanting girl

    i suspect this has nothing to do with my body

there's a lifeless horsefly in the sink   i consecrate with
        ruby blood of my moon cup
    wonder once more   what lady-like means

on the couch gran plucks a hair from her face
    it takes three tries curling under her fingernail

she catches me watching & grins

all these hairs we're not supposed to have sis!
        i laugh   *yes*
                there are always two that grow on my chin

in her chair auntie is suddenly present in the present
do i have hairs i'm not supposed to have?

i survey her ninety-four year old skin
                no they are perfect

HOURGLASS GRAINS ARE GRITTY /
IN MY ROLLS & CREASES

awed before ocean   at a temple someone else builds
       on a pendleton beach towel
    i pay too much for   i time travel in clouds

a mildewed life vest is bulky   clipped tight
     to my chest—   mandatory per gran even
         bay wading   to ankles
   i'm not digging to china
       holes don't need a purpose

   doritos bags catch sand like suit bottoms

uncle forgets i'm a girl   & lets me man
     that aluminum boat motor—
           left for right
           right for left

like the time we install more memory in the gateway 2000
     but opposite—
           righty tighty
           lefty loosey

the crab pot rope is frayed   sloppy with seaweed & my hands

can't pull the slack   fast enough

    grab from behind so you don't get pinched
        doesn't measure up—throw that one back in
      savior splashes

    i take jeffy to the swings after
        dungeness screams   a final scuttle
      a rolling boil

red-faced & short-breathed   up a dune
    in tall grass   casting future magic of when
      i will return   no longer awkward
            with a boy

  not the same boy
      from that daydream

kelp os whips   long & rippled
       against sand   seven-hundred & sixty
            eight other days   i spend
                on a beach with this man

    back to camp barefoot for another sweater
i shuck shells with gramp   yellow soup
       spills   peel out bitter lungs   pack everything in ice

        ten minutes or twenty-three years later

            under the wagon's dome light
               we raid an igloo playmate
   for kale & watermelon   until a dead battery
         needs jumped in the morning

DRIVE TWO HOURS NORTH OF SEATTLE / TO GET TO SWITZERLAND

until the purple barns
      with a few loose boards
  become more   sparse
  through the strange town *city lights*
that's almost only there for the power company
    that captures pent up dam energy &   surges it

down
      draping
            lines

to
light up the tip of the
space needle
       &   make
       sure
          there's
          enough
            wattage

        for the 'hawks to play

miles out toward   (perhaps before)   an utter void
                                    where kerouac treks to sit alone   high
in a fire watch tower   for the better part of that
                        one summer

before sweeping black ribbons
                    traversed by teeming harley stew   speakers
screaming hard rock cafe tunes
                                        into this
            cavernous
                        valley
                            half-filled
                                    with   diablo lake

past one dam just after the power-station town
& another
& another
stacked up through
the mountain pass to turn glacial melt
into welled-up
                        beryl-hued bathtubs
                                            of power

this is where we take the canoe

& we paddle out under the highway bridge
    to see what's over there back toward the calm

   because out here   it's choppy & all three of us
just ate a turkey sandwich

again in the shallows
  the tree line
    comes down— roots in crystal

     water

chiaroscuro granite cleaved by
          vapor

   ducks are laughing at us teaching their
        babies how to fly

  elders awaken in the trees—
      smoke signals up jade alp sides

i turn to the
                        center seat
                                            behind to say

i feel the people in these mountains
                                        but that's all
                                        that can be said

ancestors whisper to me

until water is fresh
                frigid under the canoe
        but salt   warm dripping at the canthi

        if i try to remember
how to tell the answers

        i forget what i arrive to ask
                            in the first place

I DECIDE THE TRICK TO DOING ANYTHING / BELIEVE I'VE DONE THIS BEFORE

ringing a campfire nu promises
         we'll remember being illuminated
     by these LED strings   he & os pass
          a smoke   beams gravel crawl
      for plots to pitch
          while nothing remains unclaimed

yuccas shadow dance memories
         of my shy role in love's silent movie—
           hunting desert monsters &
              that piano-playing man who leads us

to manifest   with the house like
    a swap meet that might open tomorrow

decades abandoned   swastikas & white power graffiti
glaring from walls

a pygmy goat with a collar
        who prances out to greet us

the prized samurai blade that's revealed
        the five gallon bucket in the garden shed
        i am pointed to when i ask for a bathroom
            a dirty dance manifest forces on love
            in daylight to a creed song

before all that manifest meets my eyes to ask
what about you? what do you do?
i lower my gaze   lacking simple explanation

he attacks instantly—
            don't cower in a corner like a kicked dog
            life's too short for that shit

but this was before & tonight
      i am pleased with my strength

i scramble easily over terrain i once would not have tried
rocks i remember require less effort   i'm clumsy
    in one crevice & (barely) scrape my forearm
        probably bruise my knee

in another place i wish i try harder   i can likely make it
    & this will be the last time
  i am scared to shift my weight

I PRAY FOR A LONG TIME BEFORE I EAT / MUSHROOMS IN MOAB

left alone   i ask for things
like harmonious relationships   & healthy teeth
the chipped one at the front aches—
                        days spent on the road

with an inquisitive tongue hell-bent   on prying out imperfection
each glossy pass obsessed   with the architectures of this
              tiny broken corner
              seeming smoother certain days

& crevassed & sharp on others—
                        maybe the whole world
                        is smoother some days

a family of silhouettes in golden hour
                is a patagonia billboard
        staged just right

i climb on a picnic table   cycle sun
                          salutations in sinking light

when i walk on the ground
                 i root down

                                  bewitched

    by the hum
                of real

TRANS-RELIGIOUS SIGNIFICANCE / SOME LONG-STRETCHING TENDENCY TOWARD HOLY

late night reading
        a wiki entry for our lady of guadalupe
while she flickers   on wicked glass tubes   repeating

glazed eyes come away knowing only
            her halo of light is meant to echo agave
& the rest is layered with indigenous meaning
        to attract 17th-century believers in polytheistic deities

when someone asks how the visions go   when i am
        twenty-four   twenty-five
        i start the story & forget to get to the point
i think this is because there are words for the context

i can say in a mirror i cease to exist
                      unlayered over & again
to reveal how the cartilage of my nose looks in a thousand
            other bodies

how i am every being whose pieces come before me
        where i come from   but also where i'm going

        some circle i can't quite yet join the ends of

i forget the disembodied touch me
        when i kick & spring up startled   again
      looking for a spider under the blanket

i forget because of their patience—   years lapse between
    that thump on the back of my head
        while both of his hands are grabbing my hips

& the tracing down my triceps
                in an empty room

I SAY HOW HAVE I MISSED THIS TRUTH SO LONG?

> *"Under ursa major, polaris, cassiopeia, a space station flashing,*
> *I said what had been said many times, important times, foolish times..."*
> —Marjorie Saiser

frozen in brilliant headlights
    along a gravel logging road—   knowing now how
        deer die in the ecstasy of being
  i say
      i know you will die too
        to the douglas fir

  i say
      how did we find each other?
        to the one next to me

& the sun sinking flashes green
      not like the legend you can blink & miss
    but in slow motion   stopped   the looming gap
      between existence & not

i step where it isn't enough to be afraid of the dark—
                         under behemoth piranhas
                    swimming in trees

the wolf dog
         who will be deaf four years from now   trots ahead
                                                     protecting me

he emanates the same green—   a halo through silver
                    beast hair

i wade thigh-high in
         galaxies water-colored   on moth wings

               we all hum toward a golden porch bulb

i take the long mossy branch i drag home
        tie on
                thirty-seven saved autumn leaves

                        matter hangs
               on white string in a perfect triangle
        i put on my wall   my shield here under
our moon   under orion   under cancer

MY HAIR SMELLS LIKE DOUBLE BUBBLE & MAPACHO

it's noonish on sunday—　　two nights in
　　　　　　　　　　　　　　　　　　one more to trek
my body restless & heavy but　　open　　&　　loose

　　　　in the joints of the knees
　　　　　　　the hips
　　　　　　　　　　between　　　my　　ribs

i want more sleep　　but it doesn't visit
　　　　i eat boiled-down broth
　　　　　　　　　　　(homemade　　none of the salt
i desperately crave)　　with rice noodles　　　& avocado
　　　　　　& cilantro
　　　　& a soft egg
　　　　　　　　　　　　i'm easily perturbed　low
on patience　　but the ends of my nerves　　aren't frayed & frail
　　　　like last year

　　　　　　　　　　　a medicine man fills
the room with loud puffs & plumes　　　　　& i bury
　　　　my nose
　　　　　　　deep in my silk scarf　　then
　　　　　　　　　　whole face in my sweater　　　away
　　　　　　　　from pungent tobacco

```
i hold it together for nausea's new wave        until i am     swept
         under its curl & splashing         in the bucket
              tears      trickle from my right eye
                    a wimpering sigh

a lady stands over me raining floral water  from her mouth   the mist
         coats my skin as i recline     empty & finally arrive—

trans-dimensional space-time traveler
                      on training wheels—

         unwinding                          weaving
                      pulsing               bright

         a minute or two in
                          not oriented      i hear

my name       low & deep         floating              i
bring
the bucket   journey on my knees five feet        as vast

                                        as the kalahari
```

right here he pats   where the fluttered ripple he disturbs
       leads me   to kneel at the foot of his mat

the first lines of chant
       pull my chin down
                       in a holy bow   of gratitude
                               open   nude

     without flesh   particularly dissolved

                       songs vibrate
my chest cavity   that doesn't even exist

                      the woman harmonizes

somewhere in the distance   it might be for all time
this happens   even though there is
                         a start & an end

somewhere in the middle
                      of forever   i ponder
                      how we get here

how these songs are mine   & how he is singing them

      how we aren't even
                                    two   things

there's another woman somewhere heaving   & i remind myself
            i am watching   *not doing*   over & over
    to what
                      begs   for a beam of my energy

                  i am watching   *not doing*

he advises this before we drink
in a response to
            a question another meditator is unable to form

just watch   while you learn how to be here
just watch

i am watching
   when this spirit & that   tempts with paths

i am watching

back on my mat   his percussive breath beats

   across the bottleneck opening
                              of sacred grit
           lulling   the medicine to sleep

       i hear

                    a breathy snore to my side

I COOK BREAKFAST TWICE / I KICK OVER COFFEE WHILE I MEDITATE

        i get up at six
                to make eggs for nu &
load the dishwasher   before burrowing back in to cuddle os
when i wake
                to make coffee & breakfast   (again)
i'm more deeply at home   in my hips
                    than since i can remember

     it's gusty—   shuffling trees
                       & making the house creak

i hug os while he's slowly   deliberately
                          putting on his sweater
right arm crooked half through   *did you just need a hug*
      at the most absolute awkward time?

i hold him hostage in the kitchen while i read verse aloud

after he leaves

      i cast a spell of protection & i shake & i writhe
& i watch my brain chide

   hey crazy
   you don't get canonized while you're alive
     there's no room for the ecstasy of saint teresa these days

i see buddha in the ceiling
      a band-aid for perceiving pure energy

somehow i kick over coffee && don't even notice until later
my puddle soaked deep
      in an afghan & white carpet

before i clean up   i sit down to historicize these things

i'm afraid i don't do a very good job of it   like saying at the end
    it was hilarious!
                        because the story telling isn't

i think of that old poem that goes perfect   after that
    other piece

            but then i think

                        how out here

    bare i'll be

IT'S DIFFERENT THIS TIME / MOVING ONLY FROM THAT SPACE

when i go to the bathroom   more to get
            out of this room
        in a place   no one can see   my face

i sit to pee & glimpse in a vision
                    two beings—two possibilities

one pulled around like a kite by winds i don't make
the other turned in to that spot at the center   unfazed

wind is on a list i see of ways to clean   energy

        i sway on a ship deck   in miles of waves—
only water for my eyes   & gales that tie bows in my hair

        i hear porch chimes
            i pause over the freeway
                    i sit on a canyon ledge

        & every time   after letting it chap my cheeks pink
            it does sweep through
                    leaves only the essential

yesterday
        when we are naked   it is different than the first time
after we meditate together   i feel the tug of the ancestors
merge them & i—
                finally encounter the edges of this body

                wandering fresh
how grateful i am   for this flesh   which i pummel
                          for too long

        it's different this time
when i grab the extra that gravity pulls

                down away

from these bones & muscles   & i smile
    at that slope

    because it's here & that makes it holy

                          i'm here

EPILOGUE

OR BACK AGAIN TO THE WAY IT'S ALWAYS BEEN

os curls up alongside me on mama's lamb skin   & nu's head
            is on my other shoulder   i open my eyes
     & projector rays splay through incense smolder—
                bob ross moving on the wall   monumental

what's for dessert? os mumbles   when i shift   *is there chocolate?*
how about that topping you put on the cake this weekend?

        is there anymore
            of that?
                           no   i say

        no baking
     no cleaning the house or going to the grocery store
all the time for doing today   i write

        he teases   *about not going to the grocery store?*

i smirk
        yes   *let me read you the epigraph*

ACKNOWLEDGMENTS

sounds in my möbius mind arose, for the greater part, throughout 2016 & 2017. Most of these poems found their beginnings in a weekly Portland Women Writers' circle lovingly facilitated by Dawn Thompson.

My work would not be what is is today without the invaluable insight of Lauren Paredes, Andrew Chenevert, Caroline Wilcox Reul & the many participating writers in Portland's Eastside Poetry Workshop where we co-create the productive space of this poet's dreams.

Deepest gratitude to Gail Wronsky & K. M. Lighthouse for their encouragement & time spent with early versions of this manuscript. To Lauren Hilger for her gentle & poignant coaching while these stories were taking form. To Love Ablan & Sierra Lisa for so many memories of magic & adventure. To Beth Melnick for her spiritual friendship & presence.

Endless affection to my Mama, Daddy, Jeffy, Gran, Gramp & all my Aunties—the ones I learned family from. To Sean & Tarek—my fam, my hearts.

ASH GOOD was born in Paradise, California, and raised in a small Oregon mill town. She is the author of *These things will never happen quite like that again* (LettersAt3AMPress) and *Years grew a keloid* (chapbook). Ash is a priestess & story teller who holds sacred space to invite all beings to connect with their highest self & healer within. She lives in Portland, Oregon.

www.ingramcontent.com/pod-product-compliance
Lightning Source LLC
Chambersburg PA
CBHW070432010526
44118CB00014B/2016